Dear Parent:

Congratulations! Your child is taking the first steps on an exciting journey. The destination? Independent reading!

STEP INTO READING® will help your child get there. The program offers books at five levels that accompany children from their first attempts at reading to reading success. Each step includes fun stories, fiction and nonfiction, and colorful art. There are also Step into Reading Sticker Books, Step into Reading Math Readers, and Step into Reading Phonics Readers— a complete literacy program with something to interest every child.

Learning to Read, Step by Step!

Ready to Read Preschool–Kindergarten
• big type and easy words • rhyme and rhythm • picture clues
For children who know the alphabet and are eager to begin reading.

Reading with Help Preschool–Grade 1
• basic vocabulary • short sentences • simple stories
For children who recognize familiar words and sound out new words with help.

Reading on Your Own Grades 1–3
• engaging characters • easy-to-follow plots • popular topics
For children who are ready to read on their own.

Reading Paragraphs Grades 2–3
• challenging vocabulary • short paragraphs • exciting stories
For newly independent readers who read simple sentences with confidence.

Ready for Chapters Grades 2–4
• chapters • longer paragraphs • full-color art
For children who want to take the plunge into chapter books but still like colorful pictures.

STEP INTO READING® is designed to give every child a successful reading experience. The grade levels are only guides. Children can progress through the steps at their own speed, developing confidence in their reading, no matter what their grade.

Remember, a lifetime love of reading starts with a single step!

Acknowledgments

*To the children of Stepney Elementary School in Monroe, Connecticut, who told me
who their favorite women athletes were through letters and a school poll.
And to principal Ronald Gustaitis and teacher Bonnie Ephraim, who organized the
vote taking and letter writing. I hope that all of the school voters
enjoy reading about their heroines in this book!*

*Thanks also to Louise Argianas, Lizbeth De Jesus, and Beryl Willett at
ABC Sports, New York Times sports columnist Harvey Araton,
Beth Albert of ESPN, University of Connecticut Assistant Women's Basketball
Coach Jamelle Elliott, and USA Gymnastics Public Relations Administrator Bob Neat.*

*Finally, a special thanks to Olympic gold medalist Donna de Varona, who helped make
it possible for little girls to grow up and become great women athletes through
Title IX, and to my editor, Joy Bean, who believed that little girls should have the
chance to read about women who had done just that.*

—D.B.

www.stepintoreading.com

Educators and librarians, for a variety of teaching tools, visit us at
www.randomhouse.com/teachers

Library of Congress Cataloging-in-Publication Data
Bailer, Darice.
Great women athletes / by Darice Bailer. p. cm. — (Step into reading. A step 5 book)
SUMMARY: Profiles contemporary women athletes, including Rebecca Lobo, Mia Hamm,
Michelle Kwan, Shannon Miller, Venus and Serena Williams, and Marion Jones.
ISBN 0-375-81186-9 (trade) — ISBN 0-375-91186-3 (lib. bdg.)
1. Athletes—United States—Biography—Juvenile literature.
2. Women athletes—United States—Biography—Juvenile literature.
[1. Athletes. 2. Women—Biography.]
I. Title. II. Series: Step into reading. Step 5 book.
GV697.A1 B317 2003 796'.082'0922—dc21 2002012255

Printed in the United States of America 13 12 11 10 9 8 7 6 5 4

STEP INTO READING, RANDOM HOUSE, and the Random House colophon are
registered trademarks of Random House, Inc.

STEP INTO READING®

STEP 5

Great Women Athletes

by
Darice Bailer

Random House 🏠 New York

INTRODUCTION

Today, girls can play any sport boys play. Girls can play on town intramural teams and on school teams, too. They even play some sports professionally. They can show off their muscles and go all out to win. And no one tells them to act like a lady.

Female athletes have come a long way.

In 1892, women who played basketball wore long skirts and long-sleeved tops.

In 1910, a woman swimmer was arrested for wearing a bathing suit that showed her legs.

At the 1912 Olympics, female swimmers competed in long woolen swimsuits—with skirts!

Being a female athlete was tough. People thought it was okay for women to compete in some sports, like gymnastics, figure skating, or swimming. But they thought other sports were too strenuous for girls.

In 1952, a woman named Eleanor Engle signed a contract to play shortstop for a minor-league men's baseball team. Eleanor could hit the ball a lot better than some of

Girls play basketball in bloomers at Western High School, Washington, D.C., in 1899.

the other players. But the team's players and managers thought she should stick to cheering.

One umpire agreed with them. "If she ever comes up to bat, I quit," the ump said.

Not many male ballplayers wanted Eleanor on the team, and she was forced to resign.

When eight-year-old Billie Jean Moffitt heard that Eleanor had to resign, she was disappointed that women couldn't be baseball players. She loved playing catch with her dad and wanted to join a team someday. Now it looked like baseball wasn't a sport Billie Jean could play.

"What sport *can* I play?" Billie Jean asked her father.

Mr. Moffitt suggested tennis.

Billie Jean tried tennis and liked it. She decided she was going to be the best tennis player in the world.

Billie Jean King plays at Wimbledon in 1966.

Billie Jean practiced every day, and coaches gave her tips to improve her game. She competed in tournaments and became one of the top players in the country. She couldn't play tennis in college, though. There was a men's tennis team but not one for women. In fact, there were very few women's college teams for *any* sport.

Billie Jean married, changed her name to Billie Jean King, and became a professional tennis player. She was happy when the U.S. passed a law in 1972 that gave women athletes an equal chance to play sports. One section of the law was called Title IX. It said schools must offer the same number of teams and scholarships to boys *and* girls.

In 1973, 55-year-old male tennis champion Bobby Riggs challenged 29-year-old Billie Jean to a match. It was called "the Battle of the Sexes." Bobby believed that any man could beat any woman at any sport. He thought he could even beat Billie Jean.

It turned out that Bobby couldn't chase down balls and return shots like Billie Jean could. She won the match easily.

*Billie Jean King and Bobby Riggs
shake hands after her victory in
the "Battle of the Sexes" match.*

Billie Jean proved that women could play sports just as well as men could, if not better!

With Title IX, girls can play any sport they want. They can grow up and become great women athletes—even topping the ones in this book!

MIA HAMM

When Mia Hamm was five, she was small for her age. Mia's mother thought she would make a cute ballerina and signed her up for ballet classes.

Mia cried. She hated ballet.

Mia wanted to play sports with her brother Garrett and other neighborhood boys. There was always a football, basketball, or soccer game going on. Mia was a born athlete and excelled at every sport. She could beat just about any boy in a running race. And in soccer, she wasn't afraid to plow through a gang of boys to score.

When Mia was ten, she played on a boys' soccer team and scored the most goals.

The boys were impressed! In seventh grade, some boys invited Mia to play wide receiver on their football team. They thought she was fast and good with the ball. They asked her to kick field goals, too.

Mia also tried basketball and baseball in high school, but soccer was her best sport. With her unbeatable speed and mighty kick, she was the best player in her state.

A U.S. women's coach saw Mia play in a national tournament. He thought she could become the best soccer player in the world and invited her to join the U.S. team. Mia did, at age 15.

The coach encouraged Mia to play for the University of North Carolina after she graduated from high school. The Tar Heels were his team—and they were the number one women's soccer team in the country.

At UNC, Mia scored more goals and had more assists than any female in the country.

UNC won four national championships with Mia's help.

After college, Mia returned to the U.S. national team. She was excited that soccer was an Olympic sport at the 1996 Olympics and that she would be a member of the U.S. team. Mia helped her teammates beat China 2–1 in the finals and bring home the gold medal!

In 1999, Mia scored her 108th goal on the U.S. team. That was more than any male or female in the world!

Two months later, Mia and her teammates made it all the way to the Women's
World Cup finals. Every one of the 90,185
tickets to the July championship was sold.
No women's sporting event had ever drawn
so big a crowd. Forty million Americans
watched the game on television. And they
were treated to a thrilling game. Neither the
U.S. nor China could score in 90 minutes of
regular game time. Neither side could score

in two 15-minute overtime periods either. Finally, the U.S. won 5–4 in a goal shoot-out.

Mia became a star. Today people scream her name when they see her play for the Washington Freedom—one of the teams in the Women's United Soccer Association. The WUSA is the first professional women's soccer league in the United States, and fans love to watch Mia score!

REBECCA LOBO

October 23, 1996. A new professional women's basketball league starts recruiting players. It is called the Women's National Basketball Association, or WNBA. The league will play in eight cities beginning in June 1997. The major television networks plan to broadcast the games live.

The New York Liberty draft a woman named Rebecca Lobo. Rebecca is thrilled. This is her childhood dream come true.

* * *

When Rebecca was growing up in Massachusetts, playing professional basketball was her dream. She hoped to join the Boston Celtics, her favorite team. Rebecca practiced shooting and dribbling for hours every day in her driveway.

When she was eight years old, Rebecca sat down and wrote a letter to the Celtics' general manager. *I want you to know I'm going to be the first girl to play for the Celtics,* she wrote.

In the 1980s, there was no professional women's basketball league. The only professional players Rebecca saw on TV were men. Dribbling on her driveway, Rebecca pretended she was Larry Bird, a star player for the Boston team.

Rebecca never received an answer from the Celtics. But in fourth grade, she started playing on an all-boys intramural team. She would have played on a girls' team, but there wasn't one!

At first, the guys on Rebecca's team weren't happy. Then Rebecca scored a few baskets and grabbed some rebounds. The boys' eyes lit up. *Hey, this girl can play!*

On her high school girls' team, Rebecca scored 62 points in one game. In four years of high school, Rebecca scored over 2,700 points. That was more than any kid in Massachusetts history—boy or girl!

Rebecca became the leading scorer at the University of Connecticut, too. During her senior year, the Huskies didn't lose one game. In April 1995, Rebecca flew to Minneapolis with her teammates for the National Collegiate Athletic Association Women's Basketball championship, the Women's Final Four. Connecticut faced the Tennessee Lady Volunteers, who had won the Final Four three times.

Rebecca was now 6'4" tall. She was Connecticut's leading shot blocker. The Lady Volunteers felt like they were shooting over a telephone pole! Rebecca easily swatted down their shots.

Connecticut took the lead. Then, eight minutes into the game, Tennessee got a break. Rebecca was charged with her third foul. Her coach sat her on the bench.

Without Rebecca, Connecticut fell behind. Then, in the second half, Rebecca went back into the game. She made four baskets in four minutes. In the final 30 seconds, Rebecca sank three foul shots for three more points.

Time ran out for Tennessee. The horn blared and the Huskies won 70–64!

After Rebecca graduated from Connecticut, she played for the U.S. at the 1996 Olympics. She was the youngest woman on the team, and with her help the U.S. won the gold medal.

After the Olympics, Rebecca moved on to the WNBA. In 1998, she led the New York Liberty in rebounds and blocked shots. But during the 1999 season, Rebecca injured her left knee twice. She missed many games. Though her knee finally healed, New York traded her to the Houston Comets in April 2002.

Rebecca was thrilled that she could keep playing. "That's what's most important to me now," she said.

Despite all the fame she has attracted, Rebecca is one of the nicest people around. She never turns down kids' requests for an autograph. She is delighted that boys and girls have women's professional basketball players to look up to. It is something she never had as a kid.

MARION JONES

Even as a little girl, Marion Jones was just about unbeatable. She played sports with her older brother, Albert, and his friends. It was embarrassing. Marion not only outshot them in basketball, she outran them in tag!

When Marion was eight years old, she played on an all-boys Little League baseball team. One day, she socked a home run. While rounding the bases, she caught up with the runner ahead of her and could have beaten him home.

Marion could run faster than just about everyone at school. Some kids called her "Flash." Others called her "Hard Nails." And she believed that she could beat *anyone*.

The 1984 Olympic Games were held in Los Angeles, California, two miles from her home. Marion started dreaming. *I want to be an Olympic champion,* Marion wrote on a little blackboard she kept in her room. She wanted to be the best there ever was, too.

Four years later, Marion watched the 1988 Olympics on television. She saw a woman named Florence Griffith-Joyner win the 100- and 200-meter dashes and the 400-meter relay. Florence set world records that year in the 100 and 200. She was the fastest woman in history. Marion wanted to run faster.

First, Marion became the fastest sprinter in high school. She won the 100 and 200 at the California state championships every year. In 1991, during her junior year, Marion ran the 200 in 22.58 seconds. No high school student in the country ever ran that fast before—or has since!

When Marion was 16, she was invited to be an alternate on an Olympic relay team at the 1992 Games in Barcelona, Spain. If her team won, she could have gotten a gold medal, even if she didn't compete. But Marion turned down the offer. She wanted to *earn* her medals!

In her senior year, Marion began to compete in the long jump. At the state championships, her jump measured 22'½"—over three times the length of a bed! Marion won the state championship and just missed beating a 13-year national record.

Marion was the best female basketball player in California, too. In 1993, after graduating from high school, she played basketball for the University of North Carolina. With Marion playing, UNC won its first national championship that season.

In the spring of her freshman year, Marion twisted her ankle on her way to track practice. Then she broke her foot the following year and missed her chance to run for the U.S. team at the 1996 Olympics. Her ankle and foot healed, and in 1997, Marion graduated from college.

In 1998, Marion competed in 37 races and won 36 of them! She made it to the 2000 Olympics and qualified to compete in five events: the 100 and 200, the long jump, and two relays. And she was determined to win gold medals in *every* event. That would make her the first athlete—male or female—to win five gold medals in track and field.

It looked like Marion could do it. At the 2000 Olympics in Sydney, Australia, she was the fastest woman in the world by far. It was breathtaking to watch her explode from the starting blocks and cross the finish line way ahead of the other runners. The 100- and 200-meter sprint races weren't even close.

Marion finished with a total of three gold and two bronze medals at the Games. Though not all of her medals were gold, she made history. No woman had ever won five track and field medals at one Olympics.

Marion isn't done, either. She hopes to earn even *more* medals at the 2004 Games in Athens, Greece!

SHANNON MILLER

July 29, 1996. Tonight is the final night of gymnastics competition at the 1996 Olympics in Atlanta, Georgia. It's Shannon Miller's last night of competition, too. She plans to retire after this meet.

At the age of 19, Shannon has accomplished a great deal. She has won more medals than any American gymnast in history. And she helped the U.S. grab its first team gold medal!

But Shannon has never won an individual Olympic gold medal, and it's the one thing she wants before calling it quits.

Shannon is introduced to the crowd

before her last performance. She's next on the balance beam—her last shot at the gold.

Shannon isn't smiling. She knows winning a gold medal will be tough. As a television announcer says, the beam is only

as wide as a videotape. And it's four feet off the ground!

Shannon's beam coach whispers a word of encouragement. Shannon nods and takes a deep breath. She stands on the springboard and prepares to go.

Shannon's chief coach, Steve Nunno, first noticed Shannon when she was nine years old. She was in Russia with a group of American gymnasts who went there to train. Shannon saw how good the Russian girls were. She wanted to be as good as them.

Back in the U.S., Shannon started training with Steve six days a week for four or five hours a day. She didn't miss a single day, even when she was sick. The hard work paid off. When Shannon was 15, she won two silver and three bronze medals at the 1992 Olympics—more than any American athlete at those games!

At the 1993 World Championships,

Shannon's back ached from all her training. She took pain pills, but they made her feel sick. Still, Shannon scored the most points on all four pieces of equipment and won the women's all-around competition. During the individual event finals, Shannon fell off the beam three times. She tried to forget about her bad performance. She focused on winning the next and final event, the floor exercise—and won!

At the 1996 Olympics, Shannon knows she can come back and win after a fall. And what better place to triumph than here in Atlanta, with thousands of Americans cheering her on? When the judges signal for her to go, Shannon springs onto the beam into a handstand. Upside down, she splits her legs and points her toes. Her next move is a handspring . . . and a backward roll. She leaps up, somersaults, and lands perfectly.

Now for Shannon's most difficult move.

It's called "the Miller," because she is the first person in the world to have performed it. Shannon whips into a back handspring. Pressing down on the beam, she splits her legs again and twists.

All that remains is a double back somersault with a full twist onto the floor. Shannon sticks the landing and bursts into a grin. Her 9.862 score will be unbeatable for gold.

"Yes!" an announcer cries. The crowd chants, "USA!" Americans jump to their feet waving red-white-and-blue flags. Shannon waves back as if to say good-bye.

After the 1996 Olympics, Shannon starts college and gets married, but she doesn't call it quits on her gymnastics career. She trains for the 2000 Olympics and does her best to make the team. But at the Olympic trials, Shannon's legs jam into the mat after a vault. She hurts her knee and falls flat on her back. Shannon pulls out of the competition in pain.

Shannon doesn't make the 2000 team. She is disappointed, but her smile soon returns. Shannon has a shining career behind her. No other American gymnast has *seven* Olympic medals!

MICHELLE KWAN

When Michelle Kwan was five years old, she started taking figure skating lessons with her older sister, Karen. Michelle thought skating was fun! She raced around the rink and felt the wind on her cheeks. She felt like she was flying.

At the end of her lessons, Michelle begged to stay on the ice.

In 1988, when Michelle was seven, she watched the Winter Olympics on television. She believed that someday she could win a gold medal in figure skating.

So, at the age of seven, Michelle began training with the Olympics in mind. She learned everything she could from her first teacher. When she was eight, she started training with a new coach. She practiced at 5:30 each morning and again after school. Getting up early was so hard that Michelle started wearing her skating outfit to bed! That way, she could hop straight into the car the next morning and save time.

When Michelle was 11, she qualified for the Junior Nationals. In order to move up to a senior level, she would need to practice more. Unfortunately, her rink was closed for hockey most of the weekend. Since she couldn't practice much there, her parents drove her to a rink named Ice Castle. It was located about 100 miles from Michelle's home. Top skaters trained there with a coach named Frank Carroll. A mother of one of the skaters saw Michelle practicing one day. Michelle was so good that the woman arranged for her to have a private lesson with Frank.

Frank saw right away that Michelle had talent. He asked Michelle to become his pupil. She was thrilled!

Michelle was still only 11, but she moved into a student cabin near the rink. She took lessons at Ice Castle three times a day.

Michelle was eager to learn everything Frank could teach her.

Michelle easily mastered jumps that older skaters performed. At 13, she became the youngest American to compete for the U.S. at the 1994 World Championships. Michelle finished eighth, but in 1995 she came back and dazzled the judges with every jump and spin. This time she won!

At the 1998 Olympics, a 15-year-old skater named Tara Lipinski won the gold medal. Michelle, who was 17, took home the silver.

After the Olympics, reporters said Michelle wasn't skating as well as she had before. They said that younger skaters were taking over the sport. Michelle wouldn't give up, though. She loved skating at 17 as much as she did at five. She wanted to keep chasing her Olympic dream—the gold medal.

In 1998, Michelle graduated from high

school, and in 1999, she started college. She still trained every day, and placed more difficult triple jumps in her program to earn higher scores. She won the 2000 U.S. Nationals and flew to France for the 2000 World Figure Skating Championships.

Michelle was determined. She was 19, but she wanted to prove she was still the best in the world.

At the 2000 World Championships, Michelle looks like an elegant rose. She skates to beautiful violin music and picks up speed.

She lands her first triple without a wobble. In the first two minutes, Michelle lands six triples. Next, she tilts her head back into a lay backspin. Her hands and fingers are positioned gracefully at her side.

Michelle is the most beautiful and graceful skater on the ice. No one can match her artistry—or her jumps.

Michelle leans her head back in a final pose. She crosses her arms when the music ends and breaks into a huge smile. She has skated a difficult program better than she has ever skated before.

Michelle is the best skater in the world that year and the next.

At the 2002 Olympics, the crowd roots for Michelle to win the gold medal. But on the last night of ladies' figure skating, 16-year-old Sarah Hughes lands seven triple jumps. Michelle backs off from one of her triples and falls on another. Yet when she finishes, she must duck from all the flowers and stuffed animals that the audience throws her way. The crowd adores Michelle—even after the judges award Sarah the gold medal and Michelle the bronze. Michelle is number one with her fans. And even without a gold medal, she is *still* one of the greatest figure skaters of all time.

VENUS AND SERENA WILLIAMS

July 4, 2000. Today is America's birthday and a historic day in Wimbledon, England. Venus Williams, 20, and her 18-year-old sister, Serena, are competing against each other for one of tennis's highest honors—the Wimbledon trophy. They are the first sisters to compete in the women's semifinals in 116 years! But only one sister can advance to the finals two days from now.

Serena is nervous. She has beaten her older sister only once.

Venus looks sad. When she was a little girl, she held a Wimbledon trophy in her hands. It belonged to tennis champion Chris

Evert Lloyd. Venus dreamed about holding her own Wimbledon trophy one day. She just wishes she didn't have to beat her little sister to make her dream come true.

If only it wasn't Serena on the other side of the net.

Venus (left) and Serena Williams.

* * *

When Venus was four years old, her father taught her how to play tennis. Venus loved the sport. One day, she hit a thousand balls and begged for more. Two years later, her father taught Serena how to play.

Growing up, Venus and Serena lived with their father, mother, and three older sisters near Los Angeles, California. The Williams family was poor. They couldn't afford to buy tennis balls, so they played with old ones they found. They played on public courts with nets that were falling down. Still, the girls practiced and dreamed.

Venus wanted to win Wimbledon, and Serena the U.S. Open. Only one black woman, Althea Gibson, had ever won those Grand Slam tournaments in over a hundred years.

"If you believe in yourself, it can happen," Mr. Williams told his daughters. The two sisters practiced their strokes, serves, and volleys up to six hours a day.

When Venus was nine, her parents signed her up for a tennis tournament. They thought seven-year-old Serena was too young. Feeling left out, Serena mailed in an entry form with her own money. Mr. and Mrs. Williams were surprised to learn whom Venus would play in the final. *It was Serena!* Venus ended up winning that competition.

Venus's family nickname is "Ace."

Serena's nickname is "Momma Smash."

The girls took lessons at a tennis academy in Florida. They listened to tips from their father and other coaches. They learned quickly and became better players every year.

When Serena was 17, she defeated Switzerland's Martina Hingis—the number one player in the world at the time—at the 1999 U.S. Open championship. Her childhood dream had come true!

*   *   *

The next year, the two sisters face each other at the Wimbledon semifinals.

At 6'1", Venus is three inches taller than Serena. With her long legs and arms, she can reach almost every ball. She has the fastest serve in women's tennis.

Serena is very muscular—and strong. The two grunt as they whack the ball back and forth.

Venus wins the first set, but Serena comes back and forces a tiebreaker in the second. Then, at match point, the net snags Serena's serve.

Venus wins! Yet it is not a happy victory for her to see her little sister lose.

Two days later, Venus defeats the number two player in the world, Lindsay Davenport, for the Wimbledon title. This time, Venus leaps into the air with joy. She has made *her* dream come true, too.